Play PRAISE
Most Requested

11 Piano Arrangements of Contemporary Worship Songs
Arranged by Tom Gerou & Victor Labenske

In the *Play Praise* series, pianists young and old will find accessible arrangements of some of the best in contemporary Christian praise and worship music. These tunes have become a familiar part of the musical fabric of contemporary praise worship.

The attractive elementary to late-elementary solo arrangements in Book 1 include rich-sounding accompaniments that can be played by a teacher, parent or an older sibling. Not only do the duet parts add harmony and rhythmic structure to the solos, they also develop ensemble performance skills.

It is best for piano students to observe the rhythms as notated, but these may be adjusted later to match what they have heard at church.

The joy found in learning these arrangements will result in performers who want to continue to *Play Praise*.

AF271011

Second Edition
Copyright © MMVII by Alfred Publishing Co., Inc.
All rights reserved.   Printed in USA.
ISBN-10: 0-7390-3899-0
ISBN-13: 978-0-7390-3899-4

Alfred

Ancient of Days

Words and Music by
Jamie Harvill and Gary Sadler
Arr. by Tom Gerou and Victor Labenske

Moderately fast, with an "island" feel

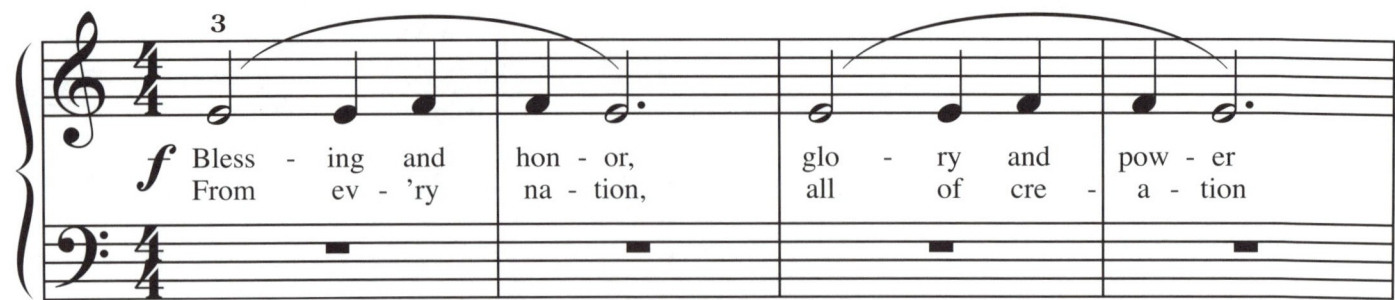

Bless - ing and   hon - or,   glo - ry and   pow - er
From   ev - 'ry   na - tion,   all   of   cre - a - tion

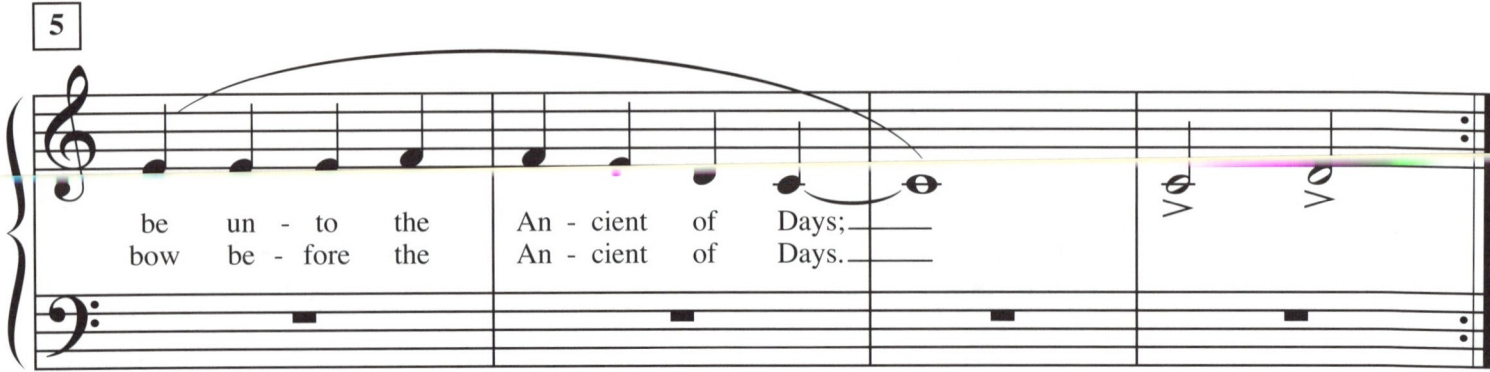

be   un - to   the   An - cient   of   Days;
bow   be - fore   the   An - cient   of   Days.

DUET PART (Student plays one octave higher than written.)

Moderately fast, with an "island" feel (♩ = ca. 176)

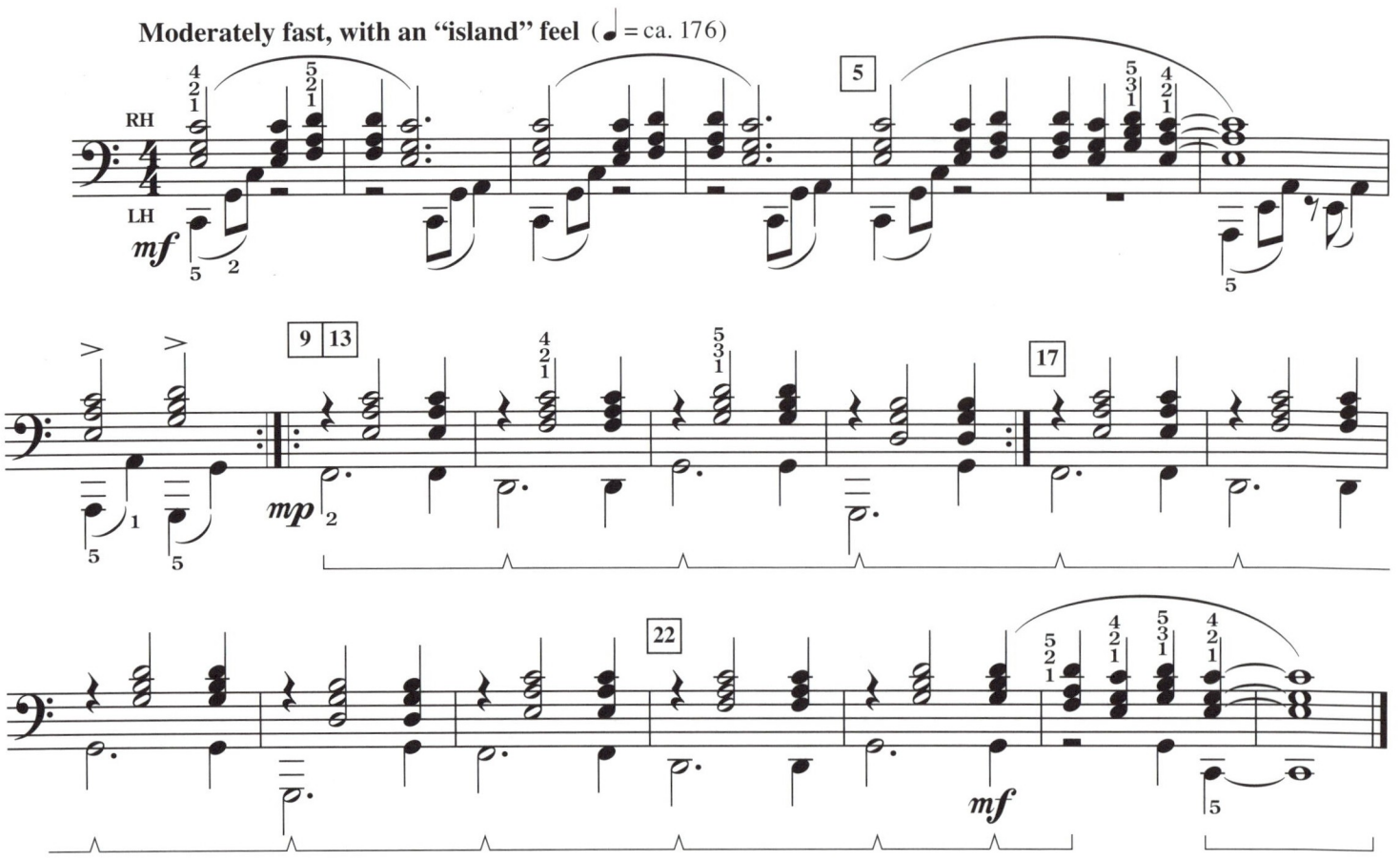

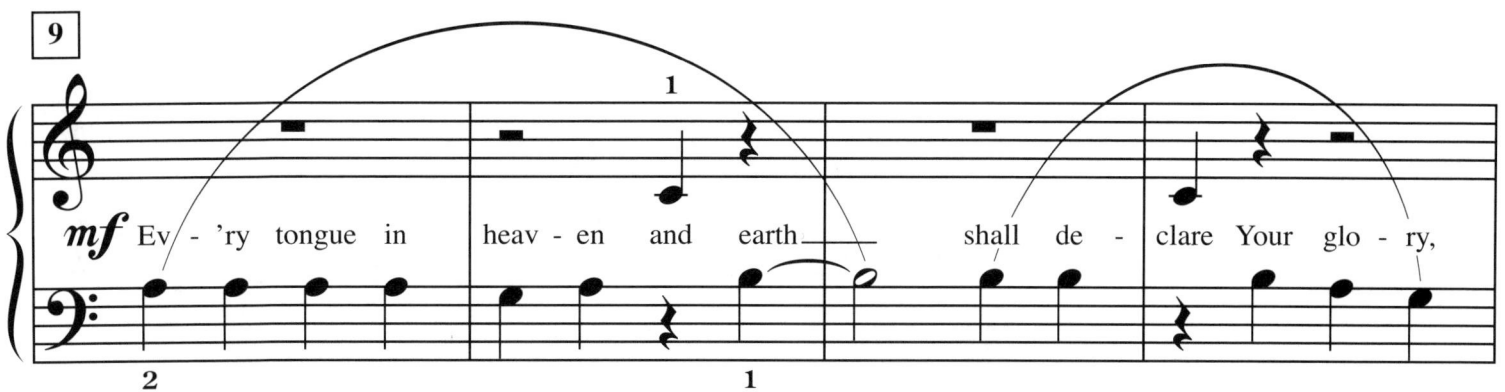

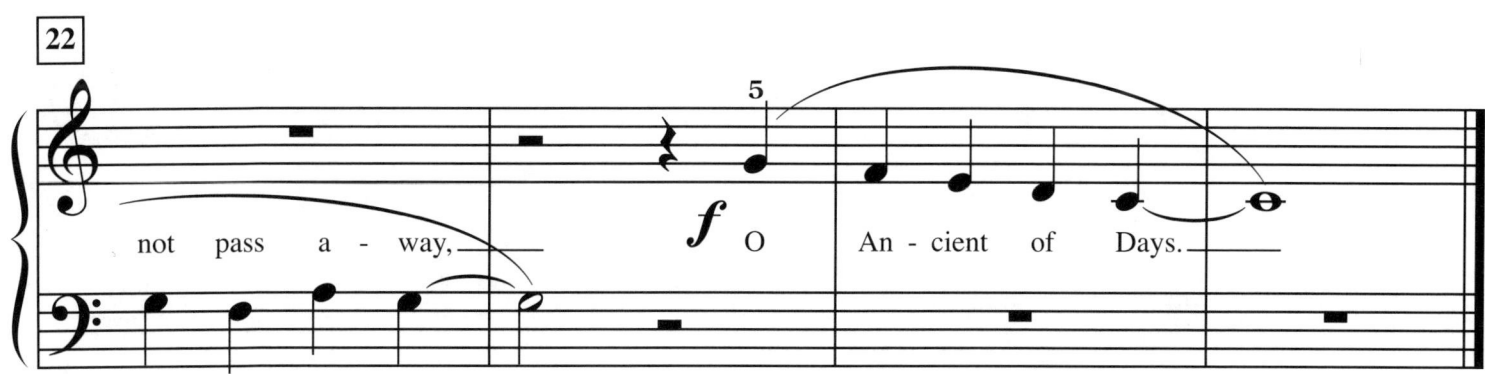

I Sing Praises

Words and Music by Terry MacAlmon
Arr. by Tom Gerou and Victor Labenske

Moderately

mf I sing prais-es to Your name, _____ O Lord,

DUET PART (Student plays one octave higher than written.)

Moderately (♩ = ca. 152)

Worthy, You Are Worthy

Words and Music by Don Moen
Arr. by Tom Gerou and Victor Labenske

Moderately slow

mf Wor - thy,_____ You are wor - thy,_____

DUET PART (Student plays one octave higher than written.)

Moderately slow (♩ = ca. 132)

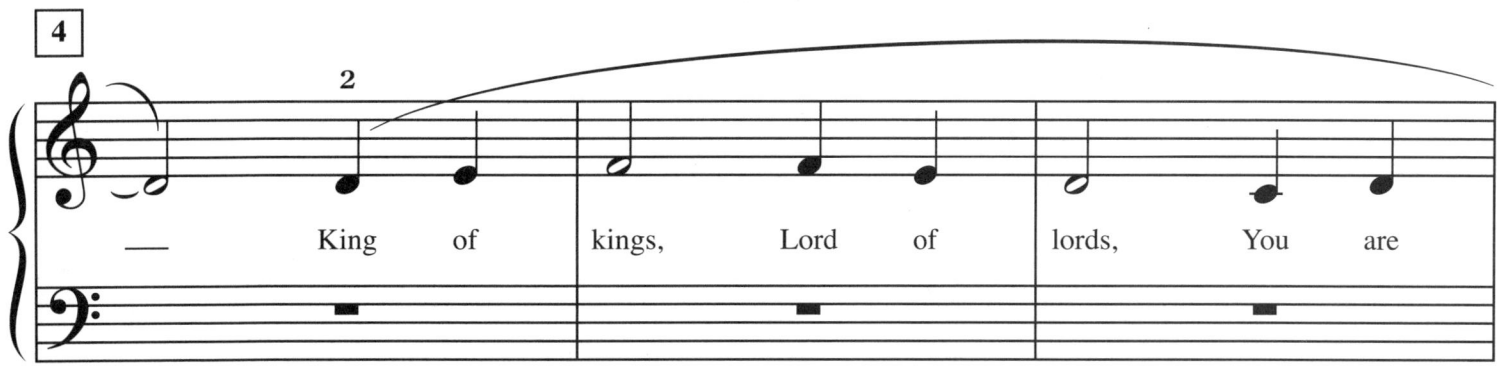

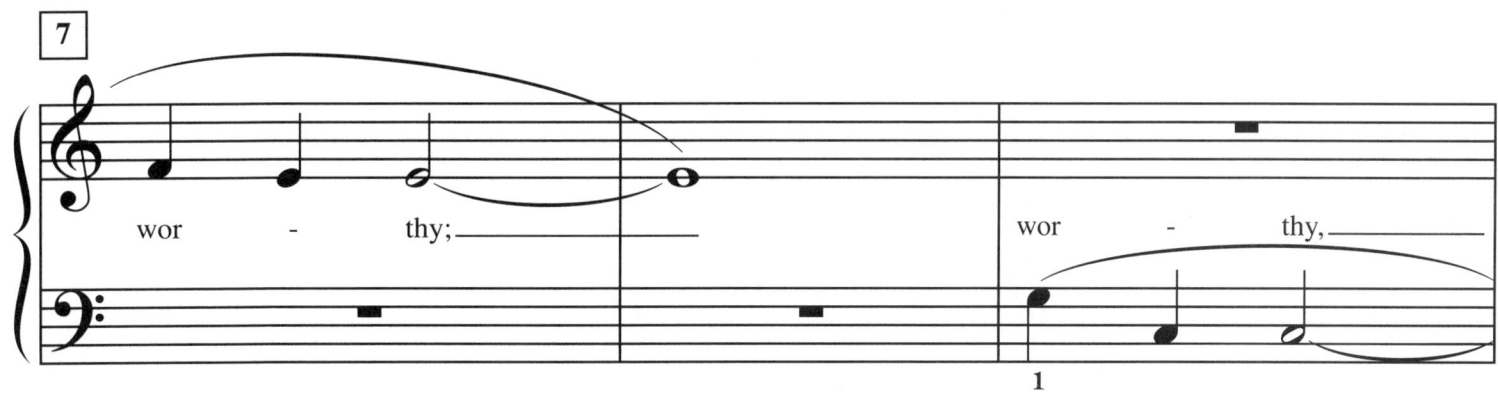

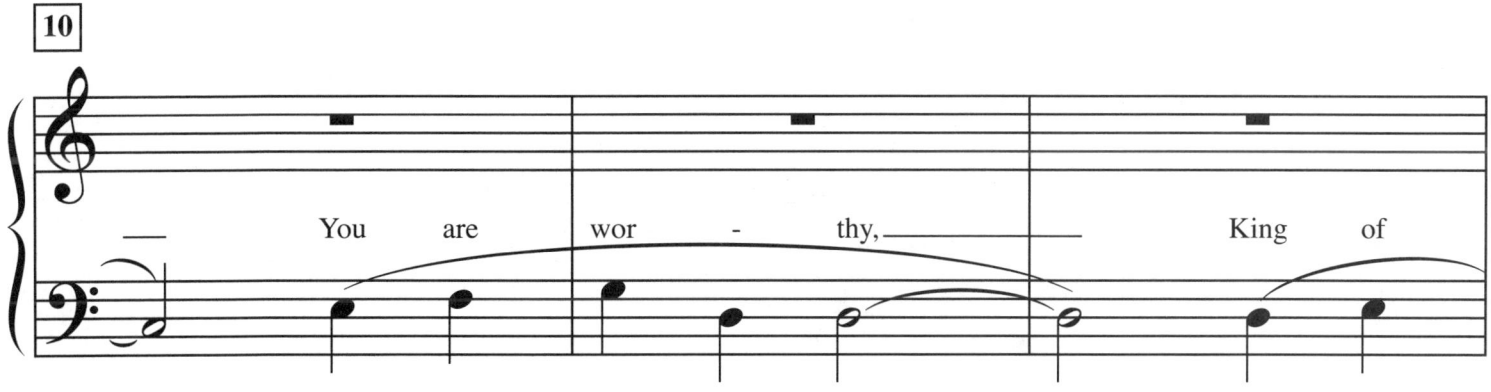

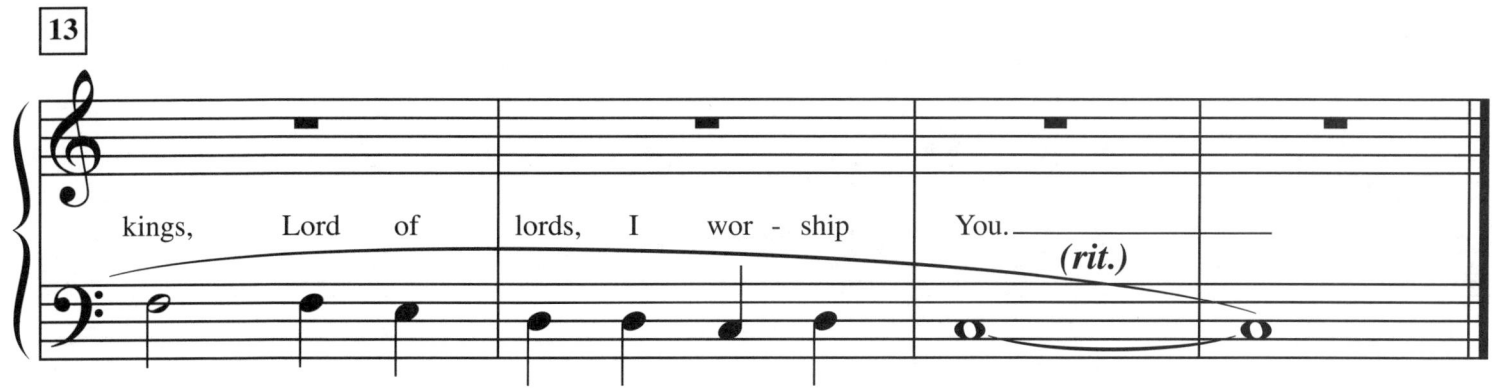

Come into His Presence

Words and Music by Lynn Baird
Arr. by Tom Gerou and Victor Labenske

With motion

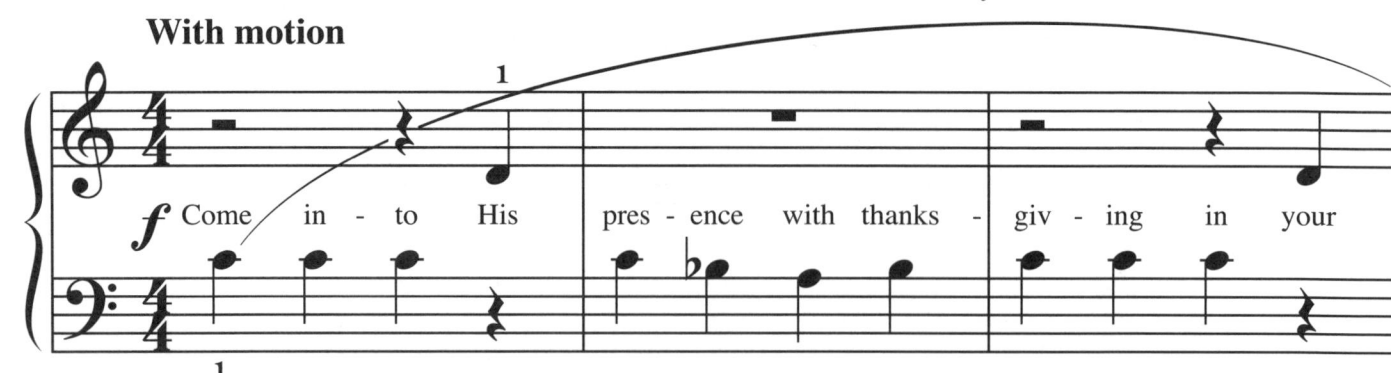

Come in - to His pres - ence with thanks - giv - ing in your

heart, and give Him praise, _____ and give Him praise.

DUET PART (Student plays one octave higher than written.)

With motion (♩ = ca. 104)

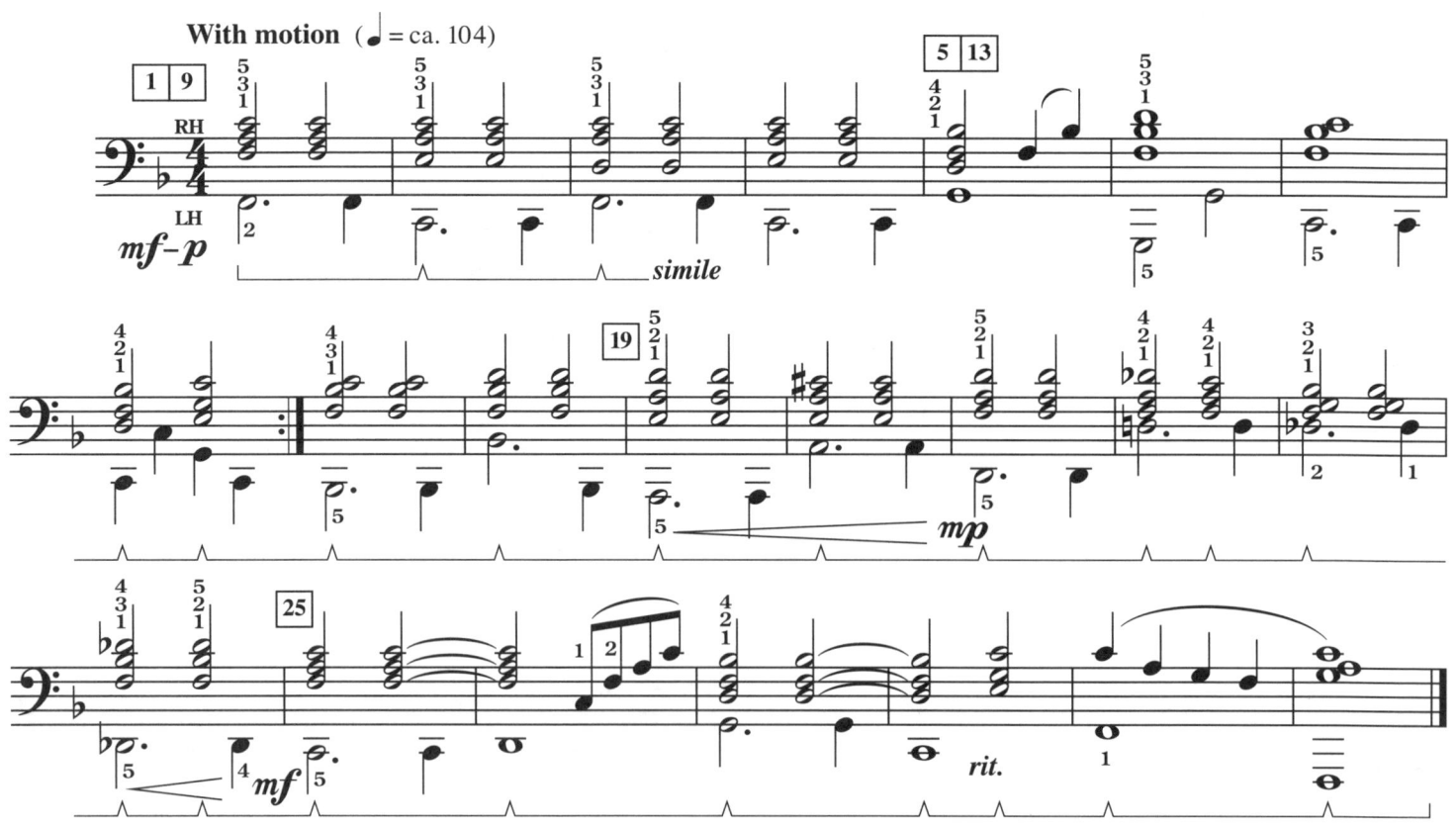

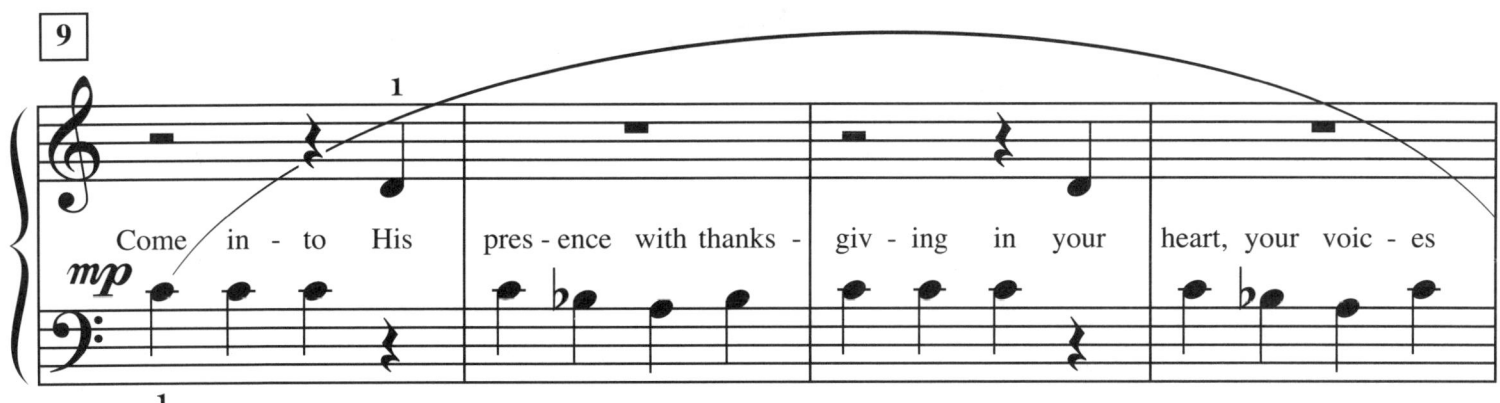

Come in - to His pres - ence with thanks - giv - ing in your heart, your voic - es

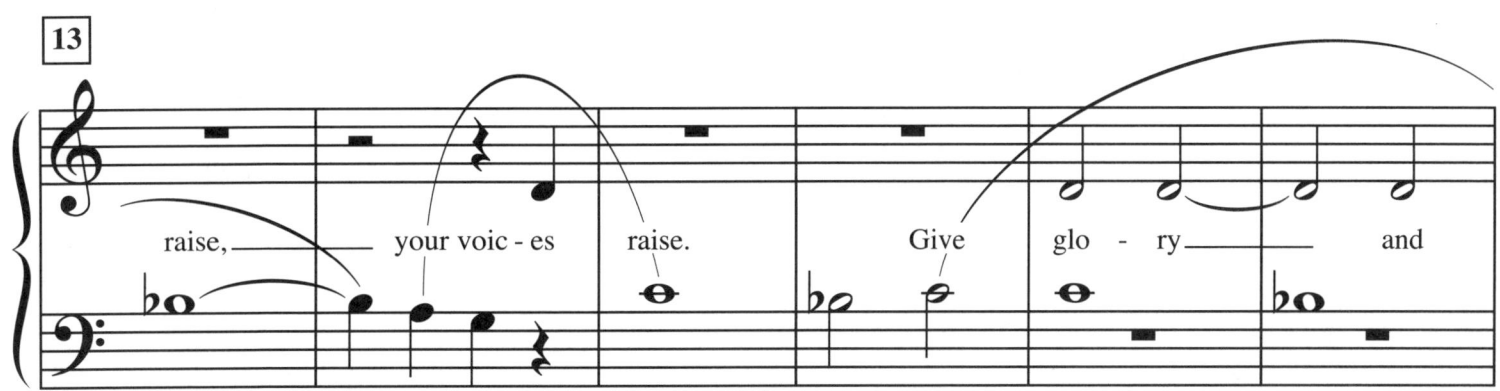

raise, your voic - es raise. Give glo - ry and

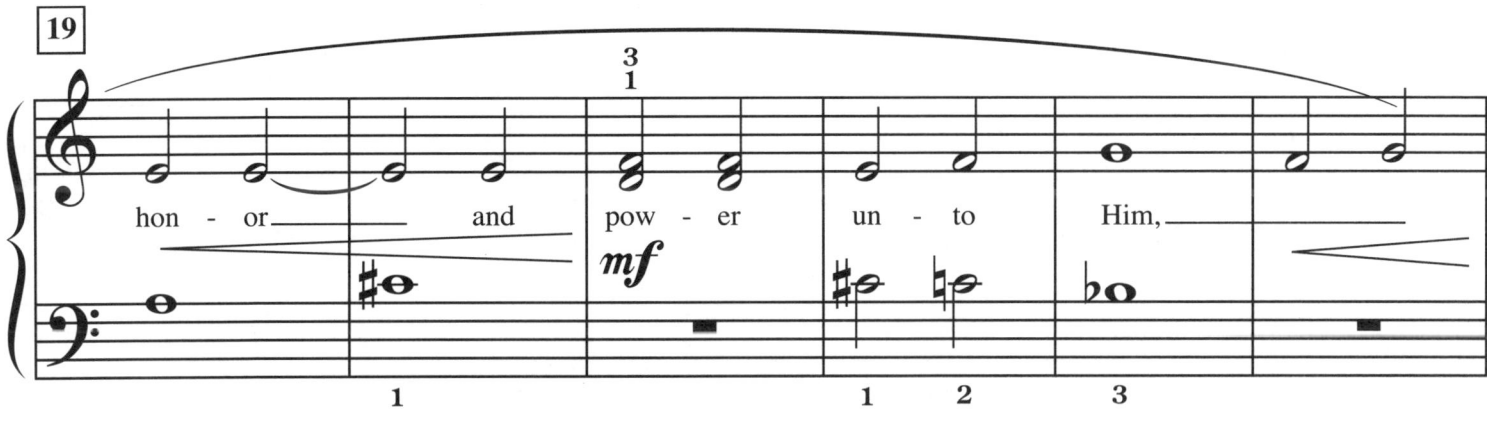

hon - or and pow - er un - to Him,

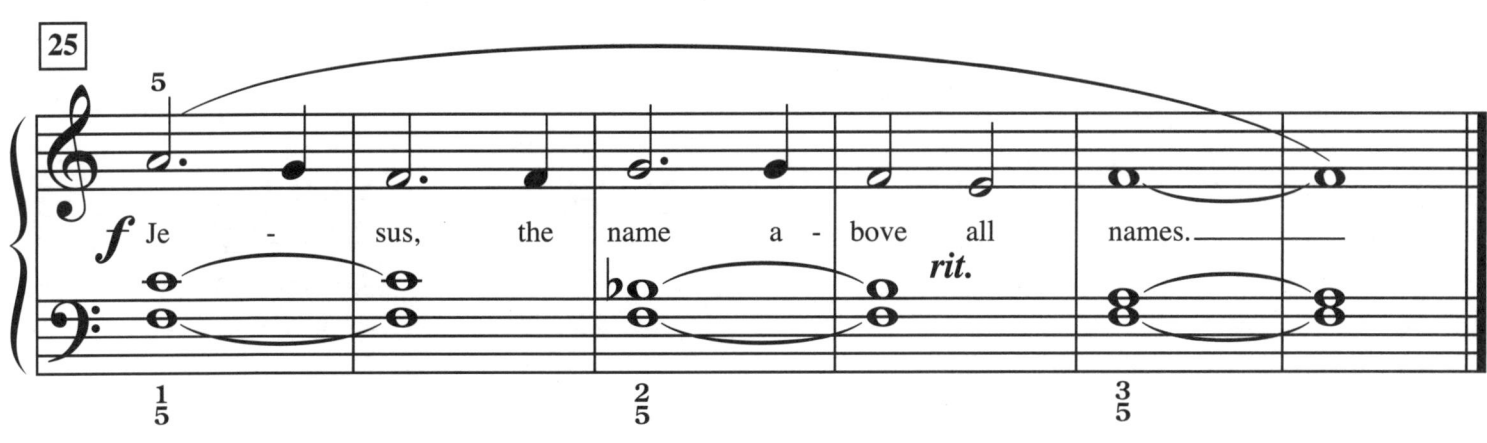

Je - sus, the name a - bove all names.

I Could Sing of Your Love Forever

Words and Music by Martin Smith
Arr. by Tom Gerou and Victor Labenske

Moderately

mf

I could sing of Your love ____ for - ev -

DUET PART (Student plays one octave higher than written.)

Moderately (♩ = ca. 144)

RH

LH

mp

rit.

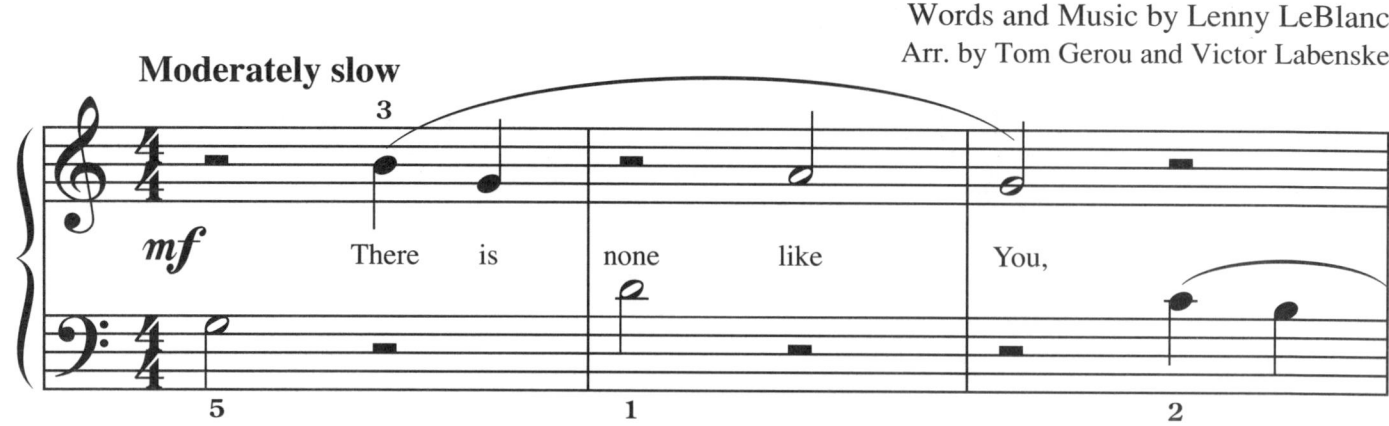

There Is None Like You

Words and Music by Lenny LeBlanc
Arr. by Tom Gerou and Victor Labenske

Moderately slow

mf
There is none like You,

DUET PART (Student plays one octave higher than written.)

Moderately slow (♩ = ca. 120)

RH
LH
mp
simile
cresc.
mf
mp
mp
rit.

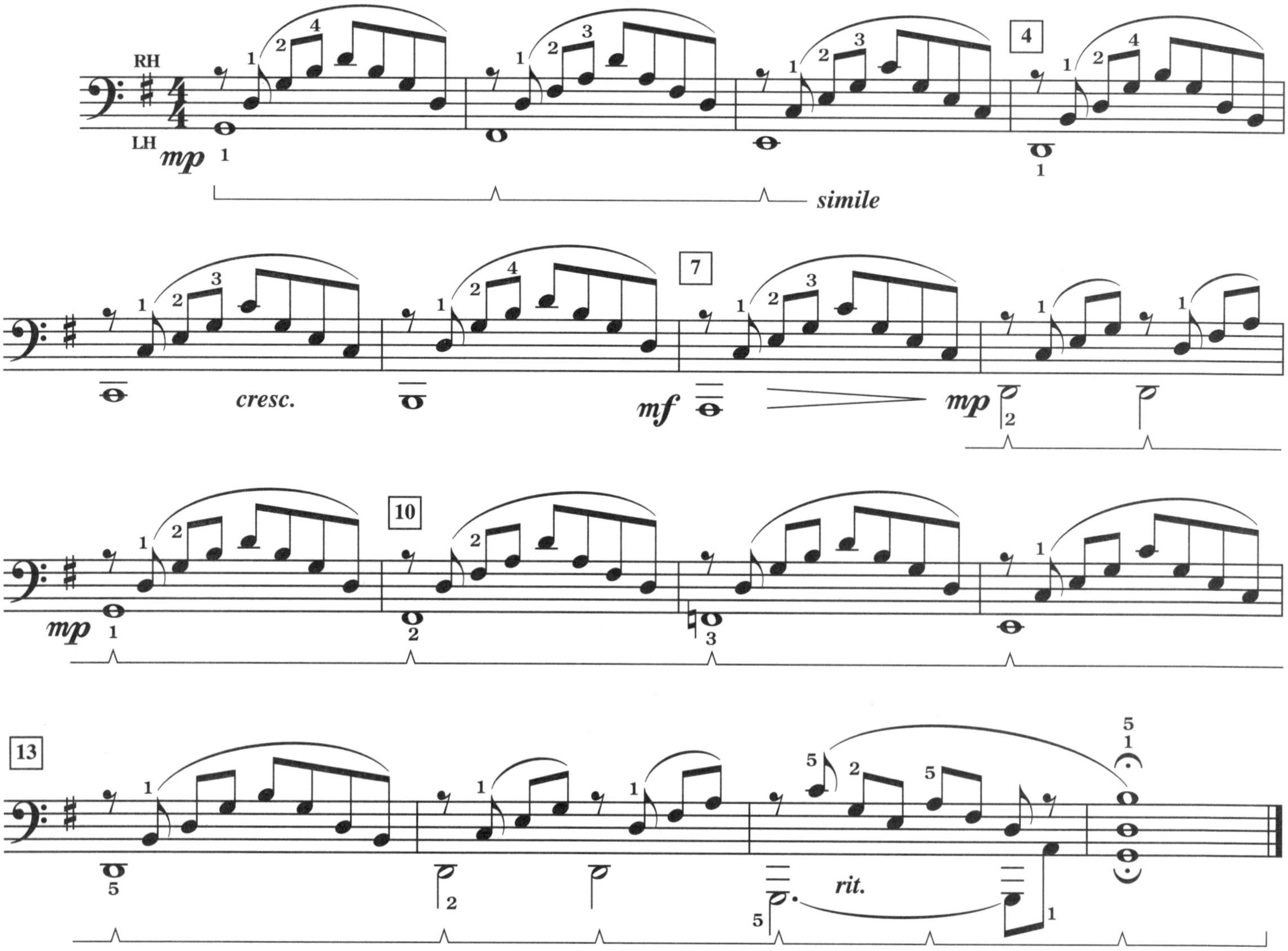

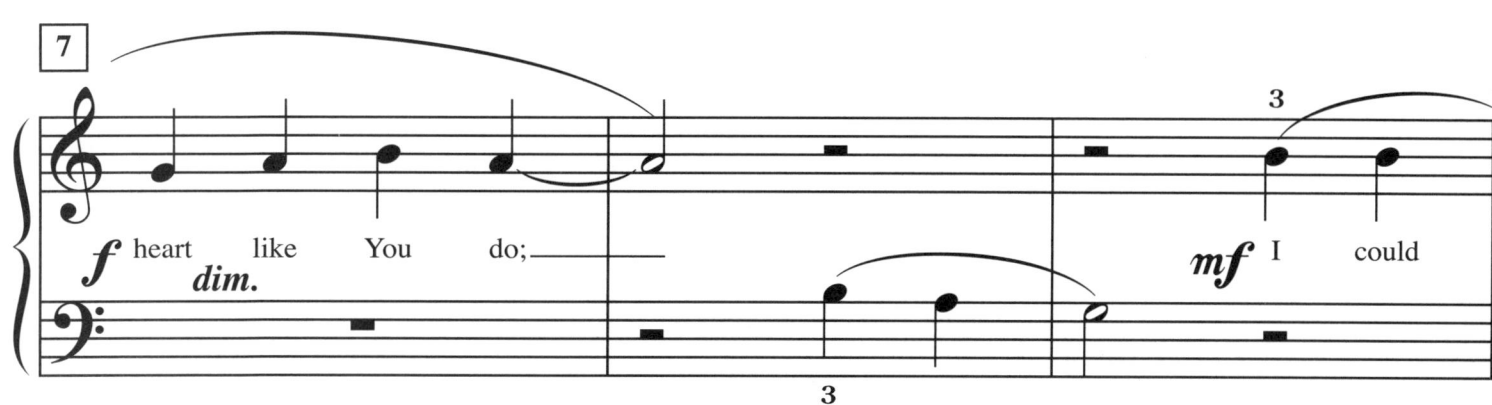

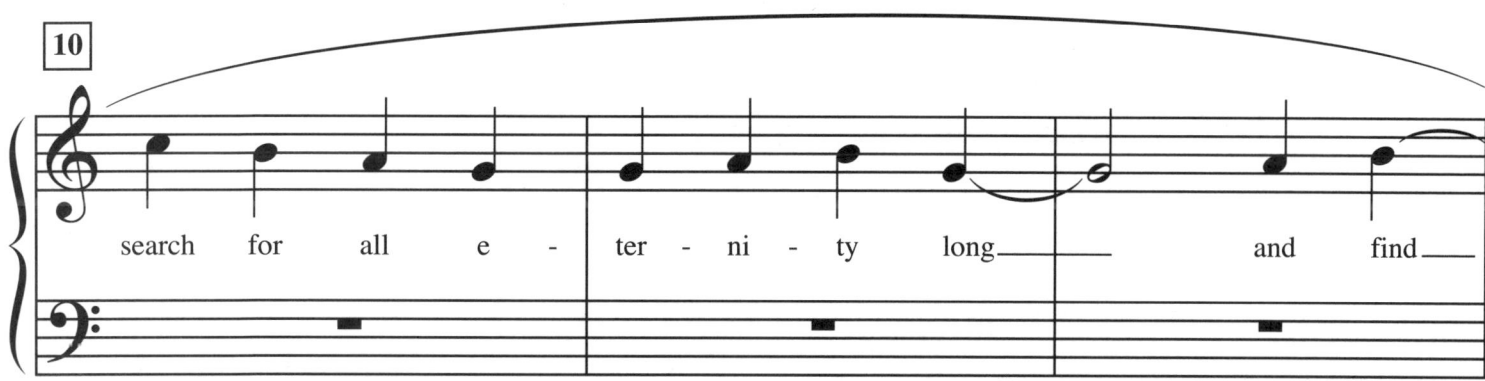

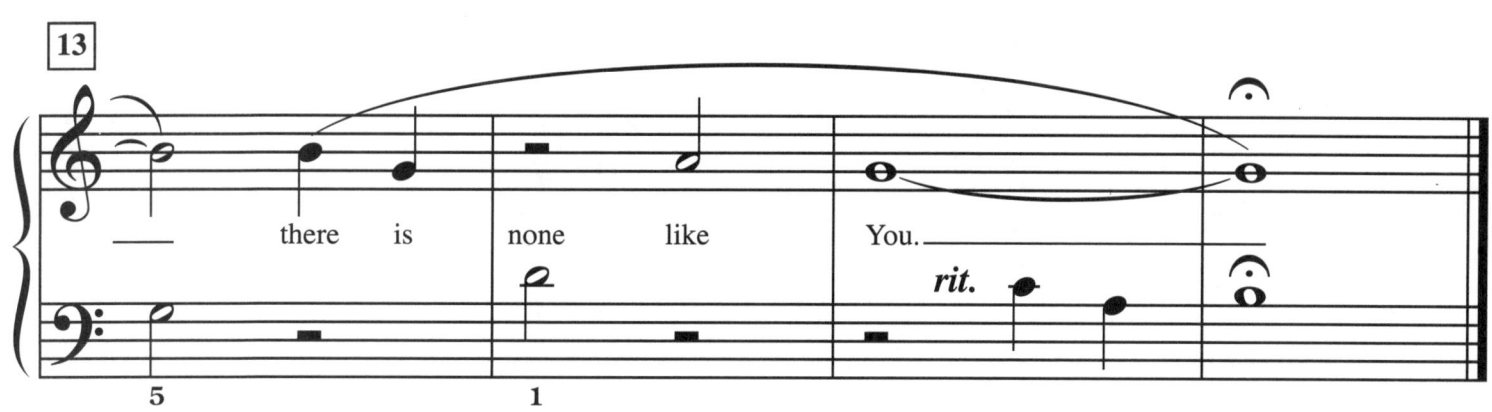

Mighty Is Our God

Words and Music by
Don Moen, Eugene Greco and Gerrit Gustafson
Arr. by Tom Gerou and Victor Labenske

Moderately fast

DUET PART (Student plays one octave higher than written.)

Words and Music by DON MOEN, EUGENE GRECO and GERRIT GUSTAFSON
© 1989 INTEGRITY'S HOSANNA! MUSIC
c/o INTEGRITY MEDIA, INC., 1000 Cody Road, Mobile, AL 36695

might - y   is   our   King;____

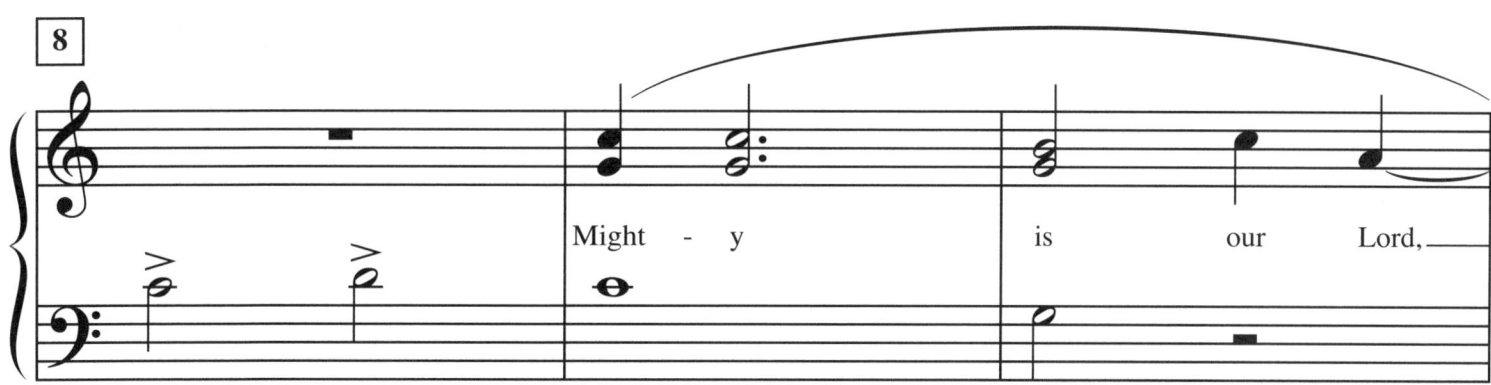

Might - y   is   our   Lord,____

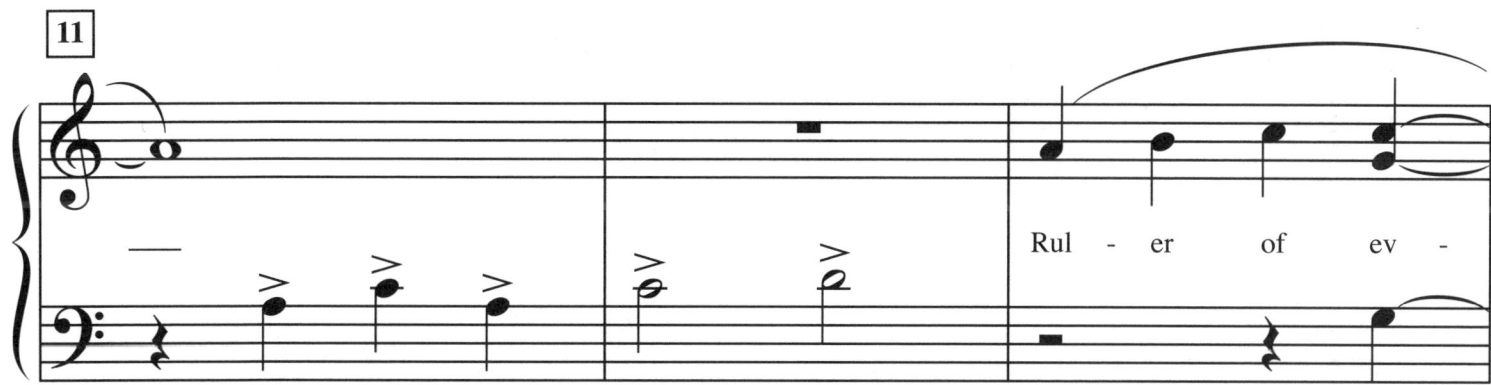

Rul - er   of   ev -

'ry -   thing.

Blessed Be the Lord God Almighty

Words and Music by Bob Fitts
Arr. by Tom Gerou and Victor Labenske

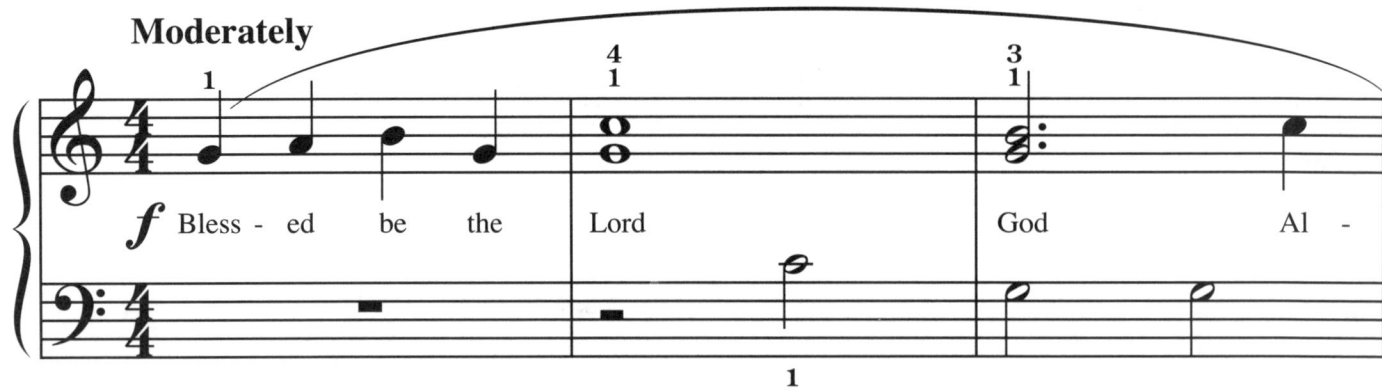

DUET PART (Student plays one octave higher than written.)

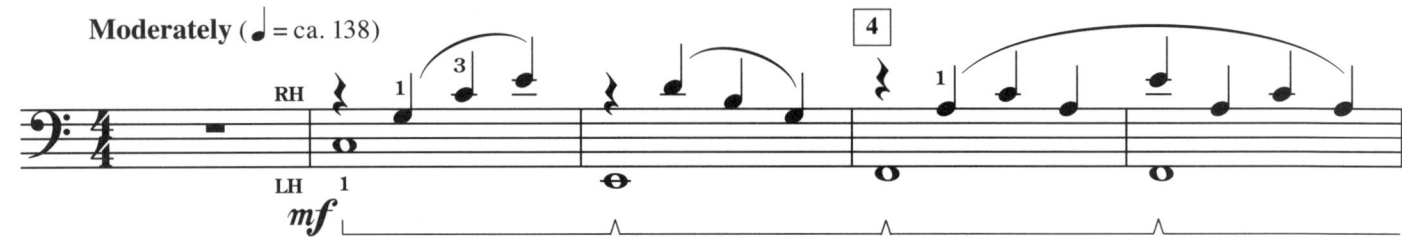

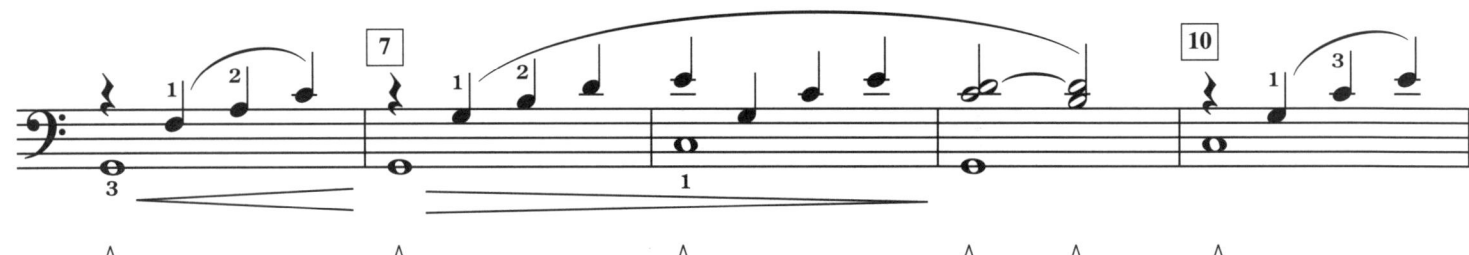

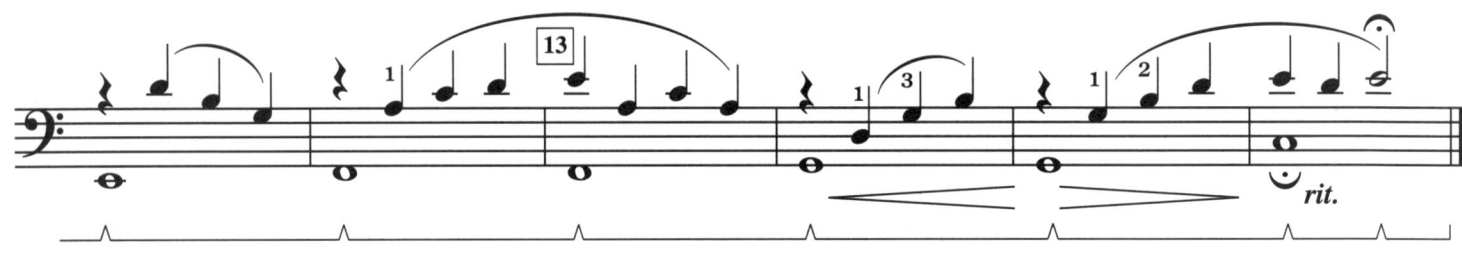

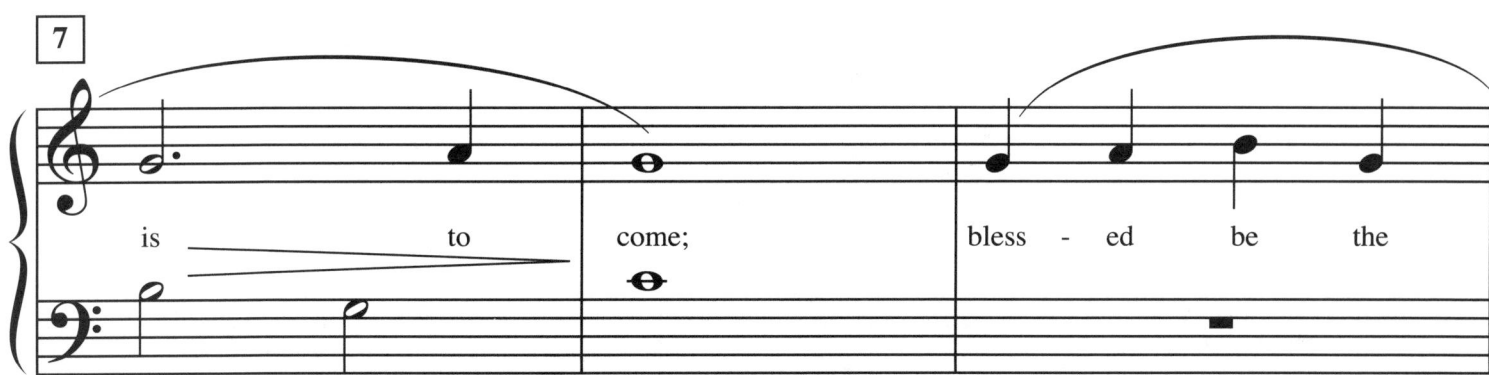

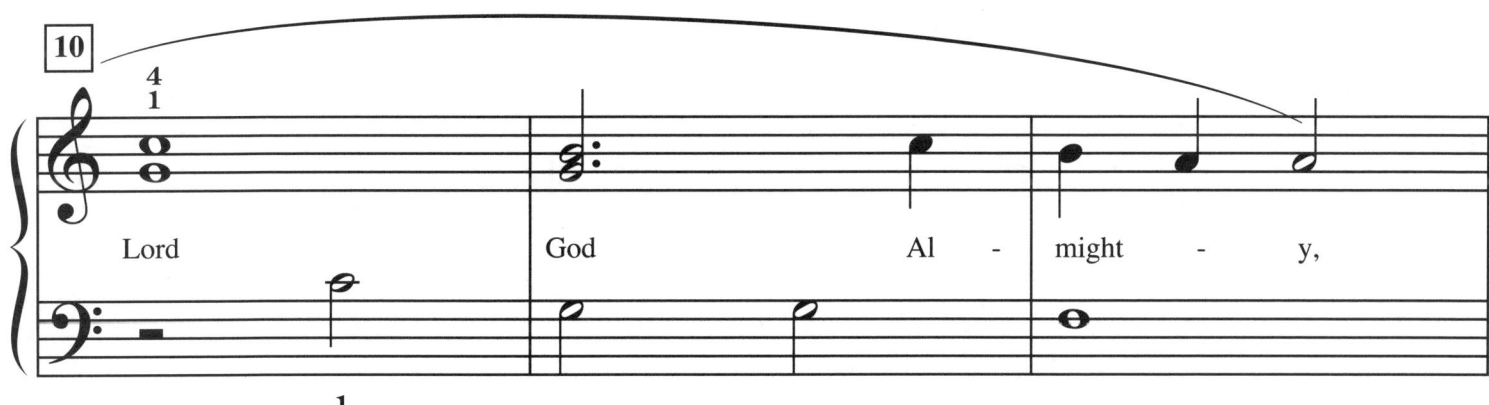

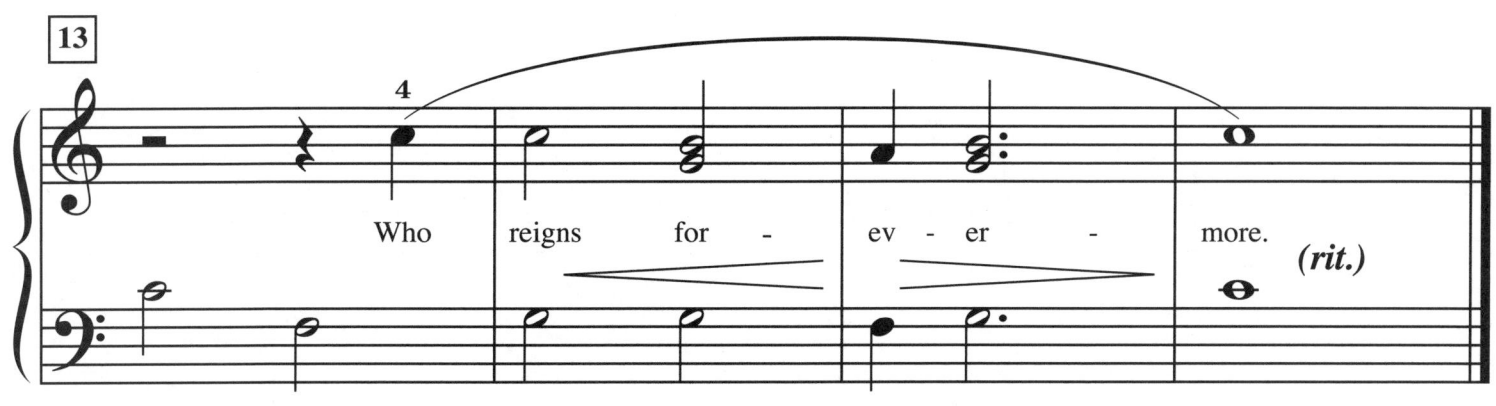

Jesus, Name Above All Names

Words and Music by Naida Hearn
Arr. by Tom Gerou and Victor Labenske

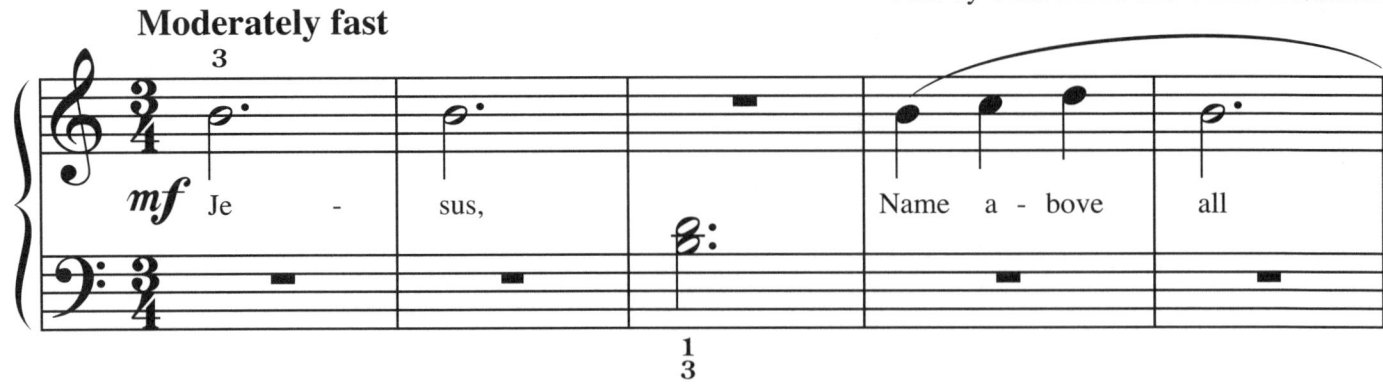

DUET PART (Student plays one octave higher than written.)

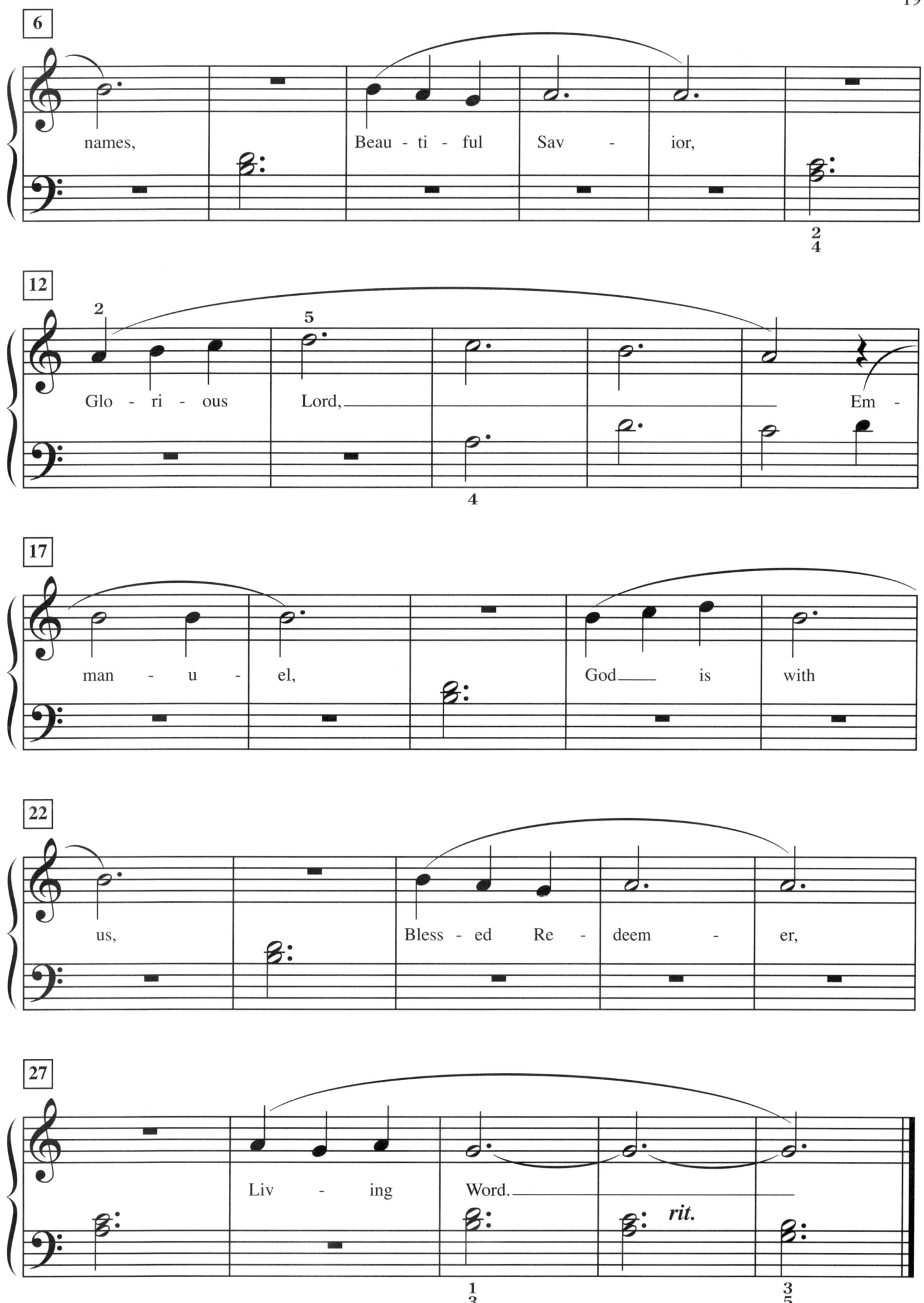

Open the Eyes of My Heart

Words and Music by Paul Baloche
Arr. by Tom Gerou and Victor Labenske

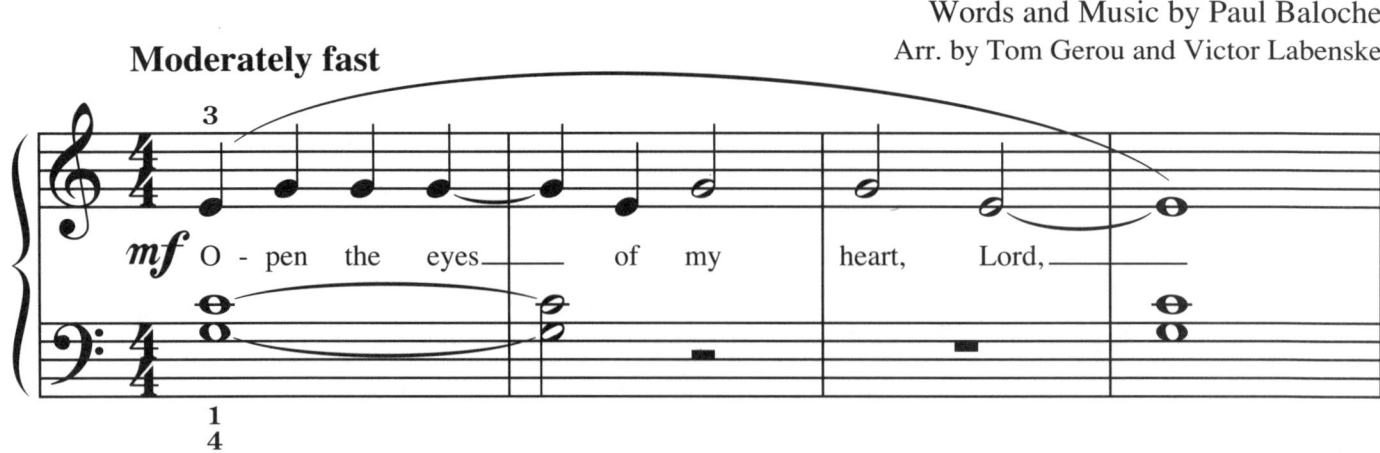

Moderately fast

mf O- pen the eyes___ of my heart, Lord, ___

DUET PART (Student plays one octave higher than written.)

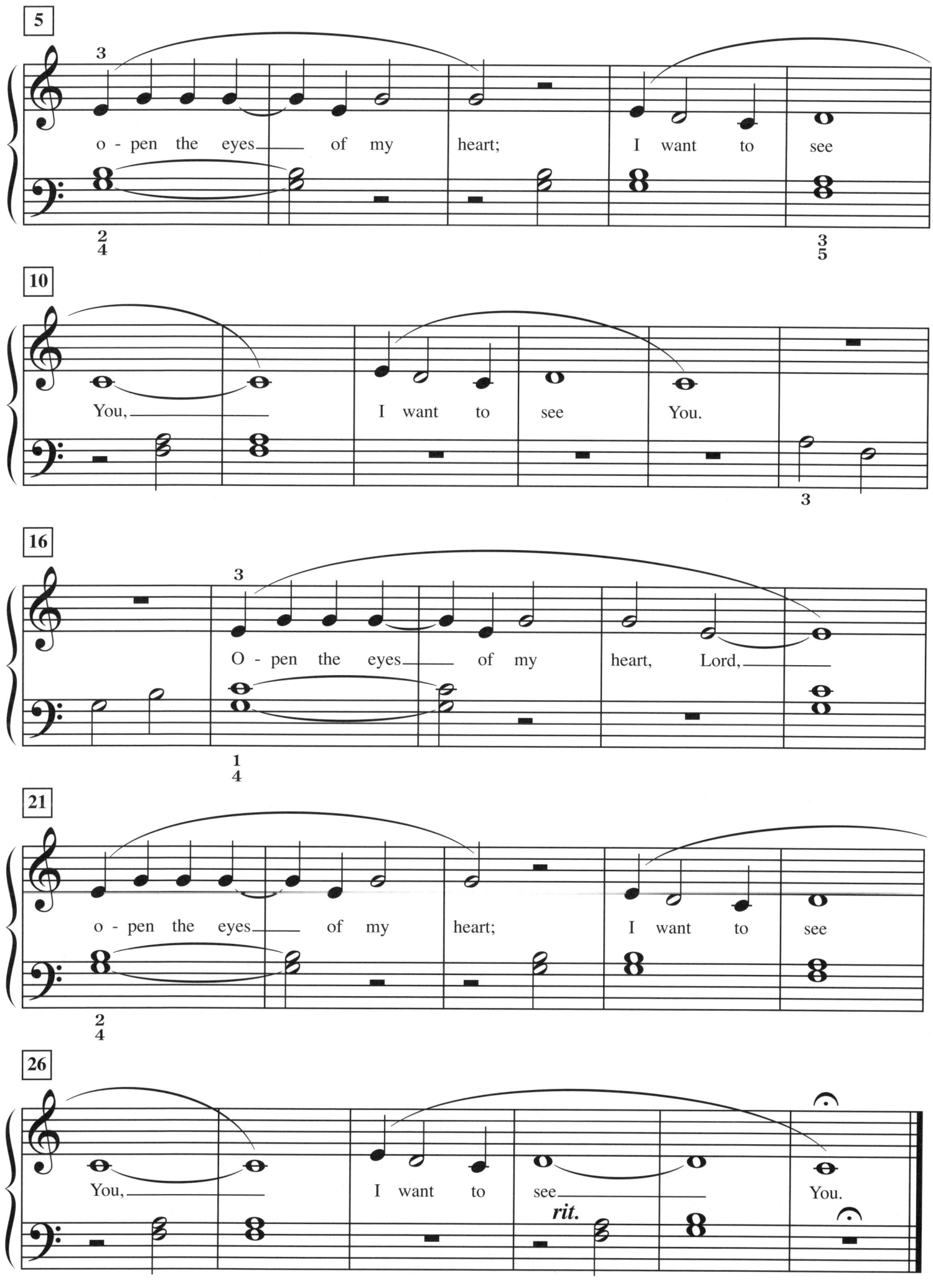

Shout to the Lord

Words and Music by Darlene Zschech
Arr. by Tom Gerou and Victor Labenske

DUET PART (Student plays one octave higher than written.)

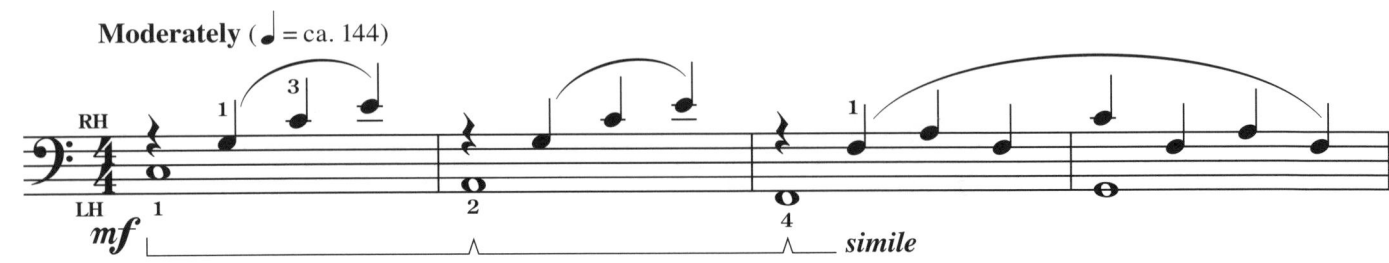

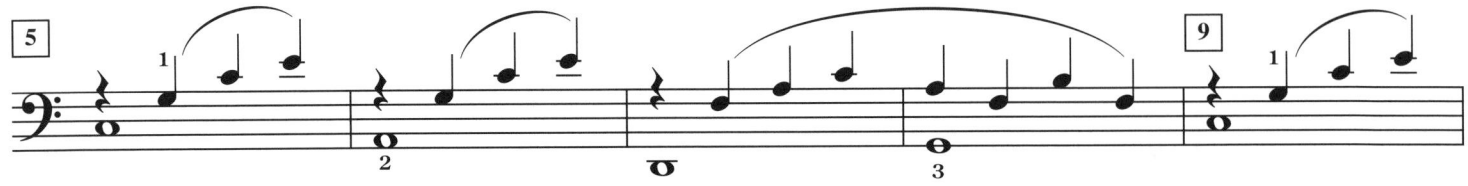

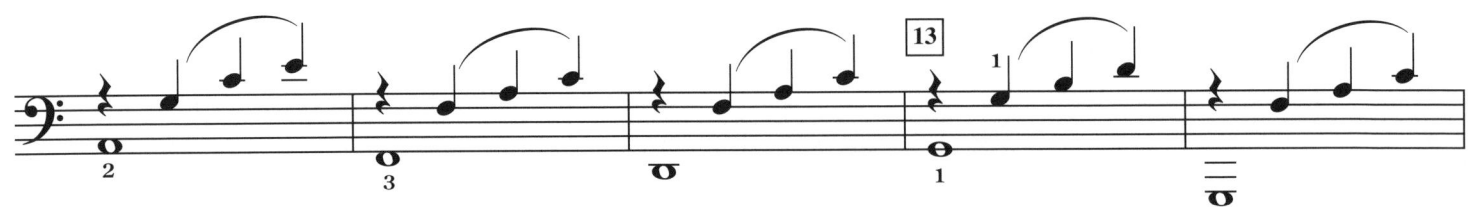

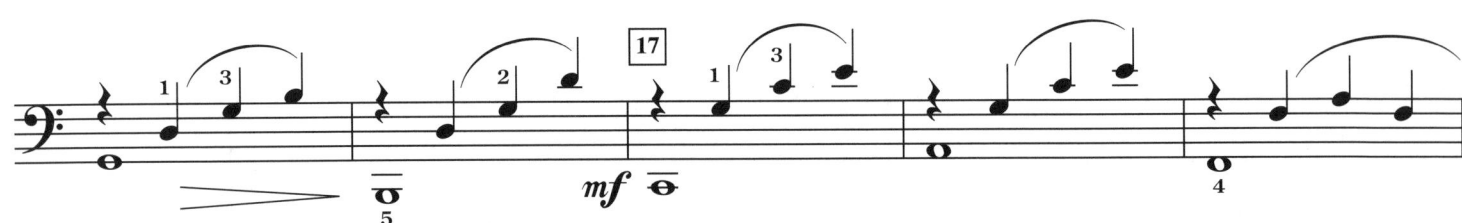

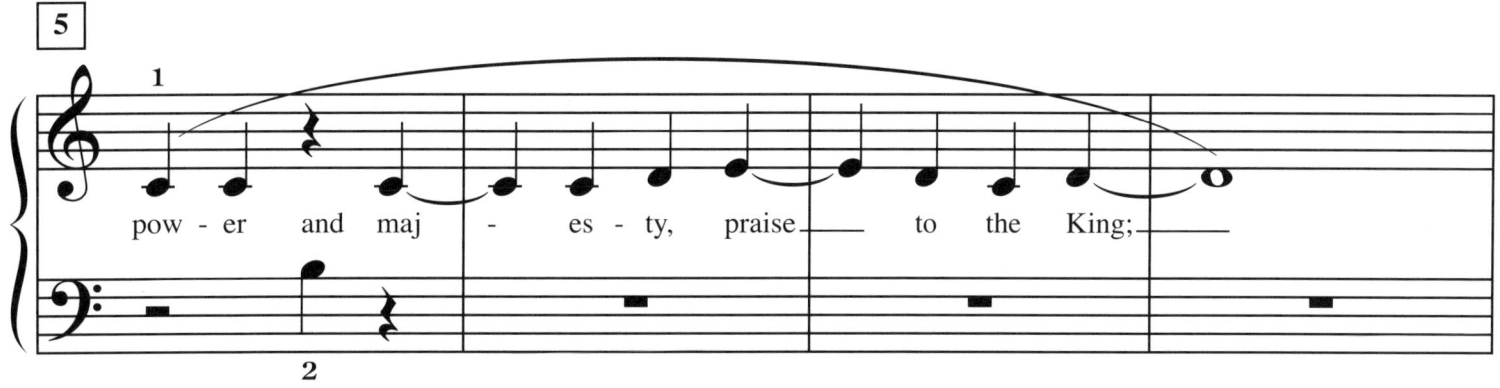

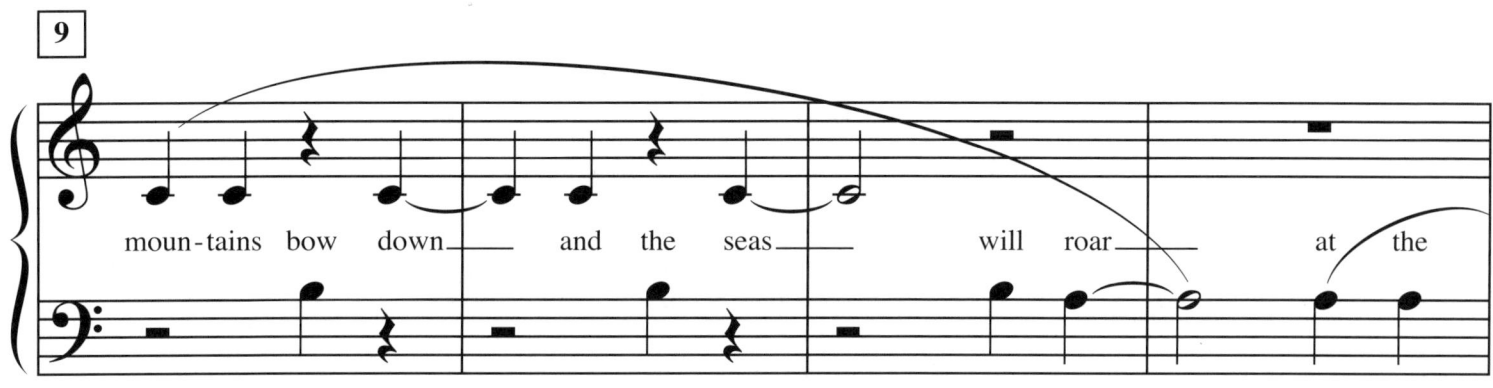

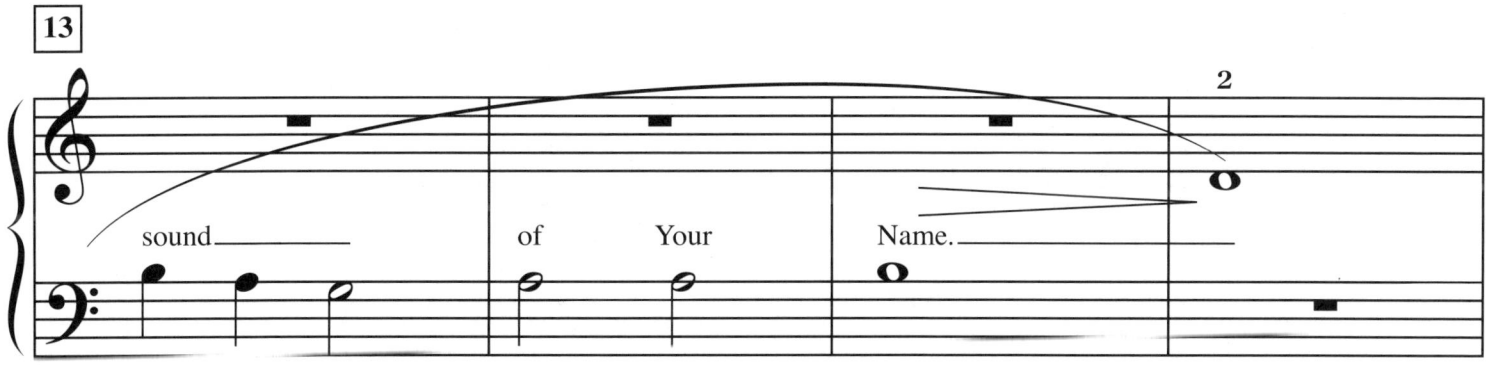

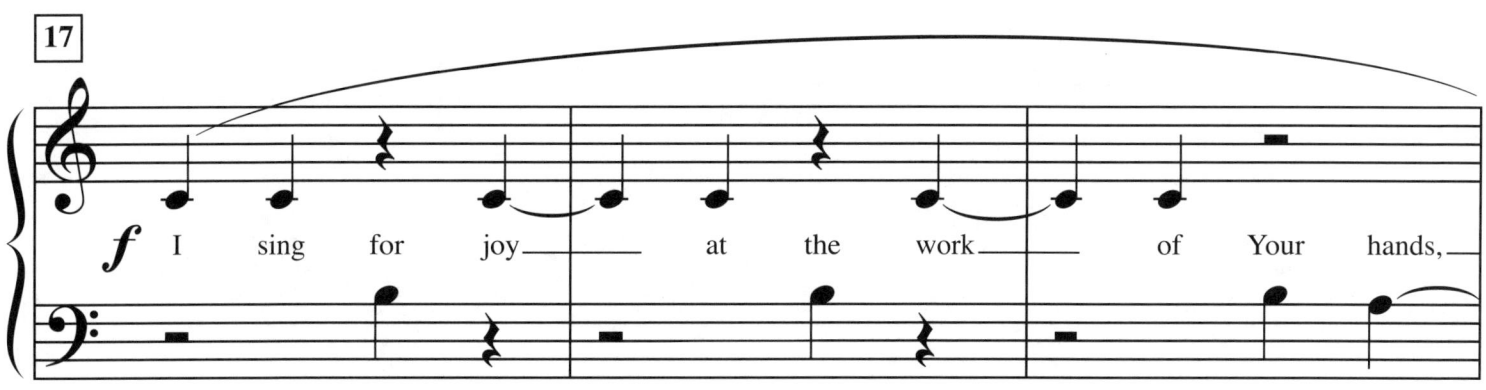

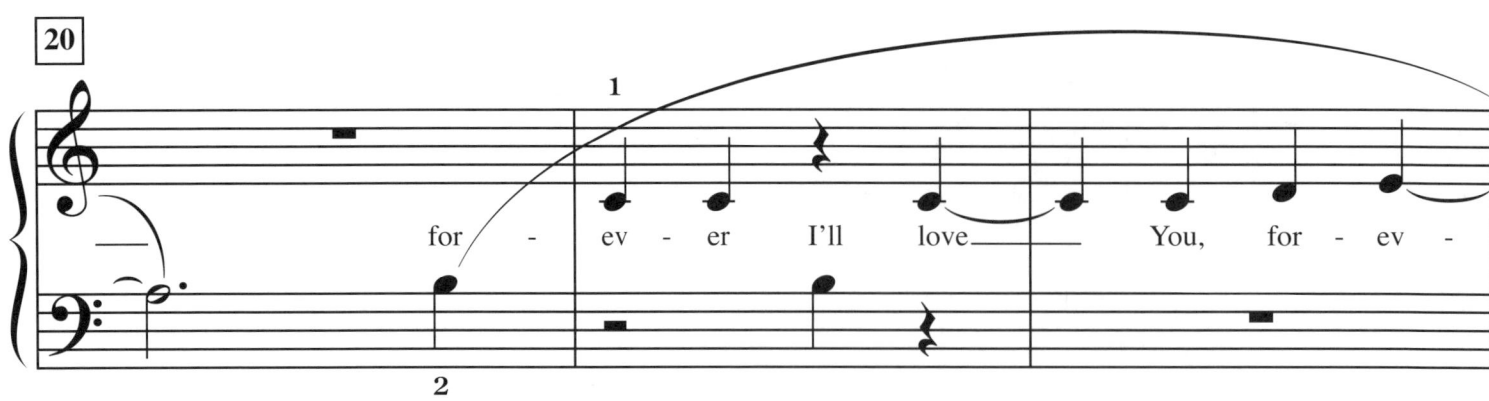

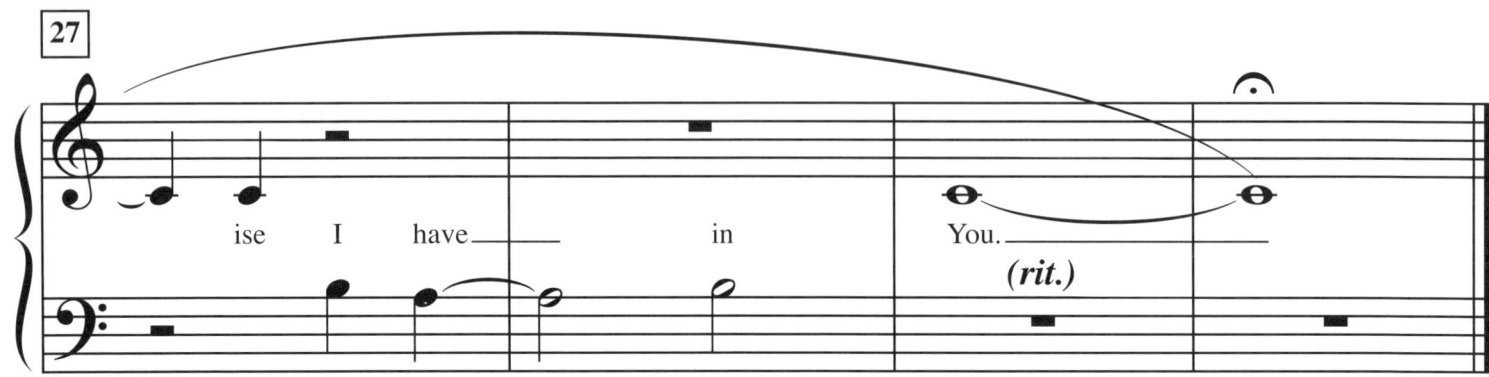

DUET PART (continued)

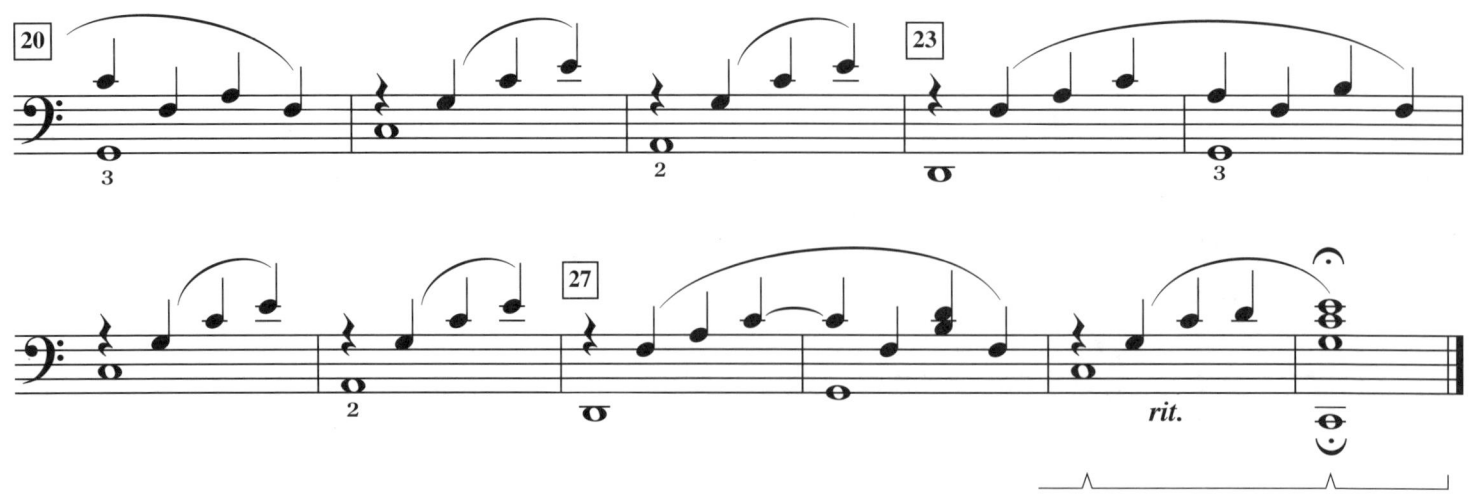